I0011176

The AI-Driven and AI-Savvy Executive

Empowering Visionary Leaders to Navigate Digital
Transformation, Harness AI Innovation, and Drive
Competitive Advantage

Silva Nash

Copyright © 2025 by Silva Nash

All Right Reserved

No part of this book may be reproduced, distributed, or transmitted in any form or by any means, including photocopying, recording, or other electronic or mechanical methods, without the prior written permission of the publisher, except in the case of brief quotations embodied in critical reviews and certain other non-commercial uses permitted by copyright law

DISCLAMER: This book is for educational purposes only.

Dedication

To the visionary leaders embracing innovation—may you harness AI
not as a replacement, but as a catalyst for greatness.
And to those who dare to lead in the age of intelligence—may your
strategy shape the future.

Why This Book?

The AI-Driven and AI-Savvy Executive isn't just another book about artificial intelligence—it's your executive roadmap to thriving in a world where AI is redefining leadership at every level. In a business landscape where disruption is constant and technology evolves faster than boardroom decisions, today's leaders can't afford to play catch-up. They must lead with clarity, vision, and strategy.

This book was written for the forward-thinking executive who wants more than buzzwords. It's for the decision-maker navigating complex change, the innovator looking to turn AI into impact, and the visionary ready to future-proof their leadership. Backed by real-world case studies, actionable insights, and expert guidance, this book arms you with the mindset, playbook, and confidence to lead in the age of intelligent transformation.

Because the future doesn't wait—and neither should you.

Acknowledgments

This book would not have been possible without the mentorship, encouragement, and collaboration of many people.

To the countless executives and innovators who shared their time, insights, and real-world experiences — you helped shape the voice of this work. Your willingness to candidly discuss your challenges and breakthroughs helped ensure that this book is rooted in reality, not theory.

A special thanks to the AI researchers, ethicists, and entrepreneurs whose pioneering work laid the foundation for much of what is discussed here. Your ongoing contributions are expanding the frontier of what's possible — and responsible — in the age of artificial intelligence.

To my editorial team, advisors, and thought partners: your guidance pushed this manuscript beyond mere content into a meaningful narrative. Thank you for believing in the importance of executive AI fluency.

And to my readers — especially the bold leaders who are not only adapting to change but shaping it — this book was written for you. I hope it meets you where you are and helps carry you to where the future is headed.

Table of Contents

Acknowledgments 5

PART 1: THE AI-DRIVEN EXECUTIVE MINDSET 9

Chapter 1: The AI Revolution: Why Executives Must Lead, Not Follow 11

Chapter 2: Lessons from Disruption – What History Teaches Us About AI's Impact 19

Chapter 3: From Uncertainty to Confidence – Developing an AI-Savvy Leadership Approach 27

PART 2: MASTERING AI-DRIVEN LEADERSHIP 33

Chapter 4: AI Demystified – What Every Executive Needs to Know 35

Chapter 5: The AI Playbook – Five Business-Critical AI Applications You Must Leverage 41

Chapter 6: The Leadership Dilemma – How AI Helps Avoid Bias and Improve Decision-Making 47

Chapter 7: From Data to Action – Accelerating Insight-Driven Decision Making 53

Chapter 8: Balancing Today and Tomorrow – Navigating AI's Short-Term and Long-Term Impact 59

Chapter 9: AI as Your Strategic Advantage – Faster, Smarter, and More Agile Leadership 65

PART 3: BUILDING AN AI-SAVVY ORGANIZATION 71

Chapter 10: Leading with Vision – Aligning AI Initiatives with Business Strategy 73

Chapter 11: The First 90 Days – How Executives Can Implement AI for Immediate Impact 79

Chapter 12: Amplifying Human Potential – AI's Role in Supercharging Team Performance 85

Chapter 13: AI and Organizational Change – Managing Transitions with Confidence 91

Chapter 14: Scaling AI – A Practical Guide to Moving from AI Adoption to AI Mastery 97

Conclusion 103

PART 1: THE AI-DRIVEN EXECUTIVE MINDSET

Chapter 1: The AI Revolution: Why Executives Must Lead, Not Follow

AI is Here—Are You Ready to Lead?

There was a time when artificial intelligence (AI) was considered a futuristic fantasy, something reserved for science fiction movies and tech labs. Fast-forward to today, and AI is no longer a distant possibility—it's embedded in our daily lives, quietly shaping the way we shop, work, and make decisions. From Amazon's personalized recommendations to Google's AI-driven search algorithms, AI is everywhere. But while consumers have embraced AI without a second thought, many business executives are still hesitant, unsure of how to harness its power.

This hesitation is a mistake—one that could cost companies their competitive edge. AI isn't just a tool; it's a strategic necessity that will define the next generation of business leaders. The question isn't whether AI will disrupt industries; it's who will lead the disruption and who will be left behind.

In the early 2000s, Blockbuster had the opportunity to buy Netflix for just $50 million. At the time, Netflix was a stuggling DVD rental service experimenting with an online platform powered by AI-driven recommendations. Blockbuster's executives laughed at the idea. They dismissed Netflix as a niche player and believed customers would always prefer walking into a store to rent movies.

Fast forward a decade — Netflix, now an AI-driven streaming powerhouse, was worth over $150 billion, while Blockbuster had filed for bankruptcy. The lesson? Executives who underestimate AI's transformative power risk irrelevance.

The AI revolution isn't coming. It's already here. And executives who want to thrive must stop following and start leading.

The Risk of Falling Behind: AI is Reshaping Every Industry

In nearly every industry, AI is no longer a futuristic luxury — it's a survival tool. Companies that integrate AI into their business models are making faster, smarter decisions, optimizing processes, and creating personalized customer experiences that traditional competitors simply can't match. Those who fail to embrace AI aren't just slowing down — they're putting themselves on a path to extinction.

Take the automotive industry, for example. For decades, traditional car manufacturers like Ford, GM, and Toyota dominated the market. Then came Tesla, a company that not only disrupted the electric vehicle industry but also leveraged AI in ways no one had before. Tesla's AI-driven self-driving technology, real-time software updates, and predictive maintenance gave it a massive competitive edge. While other car manufacturers relied on traditional production models, Tesla reinvented the driving experience. Today, Tesla's market valuation surpasses that of the next five car manufacturers combined, leaving legacy automakers scrambling to catch up.

The same pattern can be seen in healthcare. For years, medical diagnostics were dependent on human expertise alone. Then AI entered the field, revolutionizing the way diseases are detected and treated. IBM's Watson AI, for instance, has analyzed millions of medical records to help doctors make faster, more accurate diagnoses. Some hospitals quickly adopted AI-driven diagnostic tools, while others resisted change. The difference? Hospitals that embraced AI improved patient outcomes and operational efficiency, while those that hesitated faced increasing inefficiencies and lower patient satisfaction.

Even in retail, AI is changing the game. Traditional brick-and-mortar stores struggled to understand customer preferences, relying on outdated inventory models and manual decision-making. Then companies like Amazon came along, using AI-powered recommendation engines and predictive analytics to anticipate what customers want before they even know it themselves. The result? Traditional retailers that failed to adopt AI, like Sears and Toys "R" Us, collapsed, while AI-driven companies surged ahead.

These examples underscore a hard truth: AI isn't just a competitive advantage—it's the dividing line between industry leaders and industry casualties.

AI is a Leadership Imperative, Not Just a Technology Trend

One of the biggest misconceptions about AI is that it's purely a technological issue—something to be handled by IT departments or data scientists. In reality, AI is a leadership challenge. The most successful AI-driven companies aren't those with the best algorithms; they're the ones with executives who understand AI's potential and embed it into their core business strategy.

Consider Walmart. As one of the world's largest retailers, Walmart could have easily fallen behind in the age of AI-driven e-commerce. Instead, its leadership team made a strategic decision to integrate AI across its operations. The company now uses machine learning algorithms to optimize supply chains, predict inventory needs, and personalize customer recommendations. This wasn't an IT initiative — it was a leadership-driven transformation that allowed Walmart to remain competitive against digital-first companies like Amazon.

By contrast, look at Kodak. Once a giant in the photography industry, Kodak was well aware of the rise of digital photography. In fact, Kodak's own engineers developed one of the first digital cameras in the 1970s. But Kodak's executives failed to see AI and digital technology as strategic priorities. Instead of embracing the digital revolution, they clung to their legacy business model. The result? Kodak went from being an industry leader to filing for bankruptcy in 2012, while companies like Apple and Instagram, which leveraged AI-powered photo technology, took over the market.

The message is clear: Executives who view AI as just another technology trend will fall behind. Those who see it as a strategic imperative will lead their industries into the future.

How Executives Can Take the Lead in AI Adoption

AI adoption isn't about jumping on a trend—it's about making deliberate, strategic decisions that position an organization for long-term success. Executives who want to lead in the AI era must take four key steps:

1. Develop AI Literacy

You don't need to be an AI engineer to lead AI-driven transformation, but you do need to understand AI's capabilities, limitations, and strategic applications. Some of the world's top CEOs, including Microsoft's Satya Nadella and Google's Sundar Pichai, actively invest time in learning about AI trends to ensure they make informed decisions.

Action Step:

- Read AI-focused books like Prediction Machines by Ajay Agrawal or The Age of AI by Henry Kissinger.

- Attend AI leadership conferences and engage with AI experts.

2. Identify AI-Driven Business Opportunities

AI isn't just about automation—it's about unlocking new value. Instead of adopting AI for the sake of innovation, executives should pinpoint areas where AI can solve real business challenges.

For example:

- Financial services use AI for fraud detection and risk management.

- Retailers use AI to optimize pricing and personalize marketing.

- Manufacturers use AI for predictive maintenance and supply chain optimization.

Action Step:

- Conduct an AI-readiness assessment to identify areas where AI can drive the most impact.

3. Foster a Culture of AI Adoption

One of the biggest barriers to AI adoption isn't technology — it's people. Employees often fear AI will replace their jobs. Forward-thinking executives position AI as an augmentation tool rather than a replacement.

For example, when GE began integrating AI into its operations, it also launched company-wide upskilling programs, ensuring employees understood how AI could enhance their roles rather than eliminate them.

Action Step:

- Implement AI training programs to ensure employees are prepared for AI-driven transformation.

4. Form Strategic AI Partnerships

AI innovation moves fast. Rather than building everything in-house, executives can accelerate AI adoption by partnering with AI startups, research institutions, and tech firms.

For instance, Nike partnered with AI firms to develop hyper-personalized shopping experiences, enhancing customer engagement and driving sales. Similarly, Pfizer collaborates with AI-driven biotech companies to speed up drug discovery.

Action Step:

- Identify AI vendors and research institutions that align with your business goals.

AI is not just another technology wave — it's a business revolution. The executives who recognize this and act decisively will lead the future. The ones who hesitate? They'll be left behind.

The time to lead is now.

Chapter 2: Lessons from Disruption – What History Teaches Us About AI's Impact

Disruption Is Nothing New—AI Is Just the Latest Chapter

When artificial intelligence (AI) is discussed, it's often framed as an unprecedented revolution—something the world has never seen before. But while AI is groundbreaking, it's not the first disruptive force to reshape industries and economies. Throughout history, technological innovations have transformed the way businesses operate, forcing leaders to adapt or risk obsolescence.

The printing press, the steam engine, electricity, the personal computer, and the internet—all were met with skepticism, fear, and resistance at first. Yet, those who embraced these shifts didn't just survive; they thrived. The same is happening with AI today.

If history teaches us anything, it's that technological disruption creates winners and losers. Those who see the potential and move swiftly position themselves as leaders. Those who hesitate often fade into irrelevance. AI is no different. Executives who understand historical patterns of disruption can avoid past mistakes and harness AI's power to drive long-term success.

The Industrial Revolution: From Handcraft to Machines

Consider the Industrial Revolution of the late 18th and early 19th centuries. Before this era, goods were primarily made by hand. Skilled artisans controlled production, and business owners relied on manual labor. Then, mechanized factories and steam-powered machines emerged, drastically improving efficiency and reducing costs.

While some saw the potential, many business leaders resisted. Textile workers in England, known as the Luddites, famously destroyed machines out of fear that automation would take their jobs. But industrialists who embraced the change—like Richard Arkwright, who developed automated textile mills—became pioneers of a new economic era.

Fast forward to today: AI is playing a similar role. Algorithms are automating repetitive tasks, optimizing supply chains, and even making strategic business decisions. Like the Industrial Revolution, AI is shifting how work is done. The question is, will today's leaders embrace the opportunity or resist it like the Luddites?

Lesson: Resistance to technological change leads to stagnation, while early adopters gain a significant advantage. Executives must lead AI integration, not fight it.

The Rise of Electricity: Powering a New Economy

The late 19th and early 20th centuries saw the rise of electricity, another transformative technology. At the time, many businesses still relied on steam engines and manual processes. When electricity was introduced, many factory owners were skeptical. They viewed it as an unnecessary risk and expense, failing to see how it could completely revolutionize production.

Companies that switched to electric-powered machinery, however, gained an enormous competitive edge. Henry Ford's automobile assembly line, powered by electricity, allowed for mass production at an unprecedented scale. This shift made automobiles affordable for the average person, changing the transportation industry forever. Meanwhile, businesses that clung to steam power were quickly left behind.

AI is now in the same position as electricity once was — underestimated by some, but a game-changer for those who recognize its full potential. AI-powered analytics, automation, and machine learning algorithms are enabling companies to streamline operations, reduce costs, and create personalized customer experiences that weren't possible before.

Lesson: AI, like electricity, isn't just an upgrade — it's a fundamental shift that will reshape how businesses operate. Leaders who fail to see its long-term potential will struggle to compete.

The Internet Boom: Winners and Losers of the Digital Age

Perhaps the most recent and striking parallel to AI is the rise of the internet in the 1990s and early 2000s. Initially, many business executives dismissed the internet as a trend. Some of the biggest brands in retail, media, and finance failed to adapt. Others saw the shift coming and seized the moment.

One of the best examples of this is Jeff Bezos and Amazon. In the mid-1990s, Bezos recognized that e-commerce would revolutionize retail. While major brick-and-mortar retailers ignored online shopping, Bezos built Amazon with a digital-first approach. Today, Amazon is a trillion-dollar company, while many of its former competitors — Sears, Toys "R" Us, and Borders — went bankrupt.

Compare that to Blockbuster, the video rental giant that had every opportunity to pivot in the face of online streaming. Netflix, a small competitor at the time, built its platform using AI-powered recommendations and on-demand digital streaming. Blockbuster had the chance to acquire Netflix for just $50 million, but its executives laughed off the idea. They didn't believe the internet and AI-powered content curation would replace physical rental stores.

We know how that story ended — Netflix is now worth over $200 billion, and Blockbuster is a distant memory.

Lesson: Every major technological revolution creates a new set of winners and losers. The key difference? Visionary leaders who embrace change and invest in emerging technologies versus those who dismiss them.

AI's Role in Today's Business World: The Next Frontier of Disruption

AI is not just another tool—it's a paradigm shift, much like the Industrial Revolution, the rise of electricity, and the internet era. It's already transforming industries at an accelerated pace:

- Finance: AI is used in fraud detection, risk management, and algorithmic trading, giving financial institutions a competitive edge.

- Healthcare: AI-powered diagnostics can detect diseases like cancer earlier and more accurately than human doctors alone.

- Retail: AI-driven chatbots, personalization engines, and supply chain optimizations are helping retailers improve efficiency and customer satisfaction.

- Manufacturing: Predictive maintenance powered by AI is reducing downtime and cutting costs for industrial companies.

The key takeaway? AI isn't coming—it's already here.

Lesson: Executives must act now. AI is evolving rapidly, and those who hesitate will find themselves playing catch-up, just like the businesses that resisted previous technological revolutions.

How Executives Can Avoid the Mistakes of the Past

If history repeats itself, then executives must learn from past disruptions to successfully navigate AI's impact. Here's how:

1. Don't Wait—Adopt AI Early

One of the biggest mistakes companies made during previous technological shifts was waiting too long to adapt. Executives should start integrating AI now, even if it's in small steps.

✓ Actionable Step: Invest in AI tools that improve efficiency, such as automation software, AI-driven analytics, and chatbots.

2. Develop an AI-Ready Workforce

Just as companies had to train employees to work with machines during the Industrial Revolution, today's businesses must reskill and upskill their teams to work alongside AI.

✓ Actionable Step: Implement AI training programs for employees, ensuring they understand how AI will enhance their roles rather than replace them.

3. Experiment and Innovate

Netflix, Amazon, and Tesla all became industry leaders by experimenting with new technologies before their competitors did. AI presents a similar opportunity — executives must be willing to test and iterate.

✓ Actionable Step: Create an AI innovation lab within your company to explore AI-driven solutions for customer experience, operations, and decision-making.

4. Challenge Legacy Thinking

Kodak, Blockbuster, and Borders all suffered because their executives couldn't break free from outdated business models. The biggest danger for today's leaders? Clinging to old ways of doing business.

✓ Actionable Step: Regularly assess whether traditional business strategies still make sense in an AI-driven world. Be willing to pivot when necessary.

The Future Belongs to AI-Driven Leaders

History has shown that every major technological disruption brings fear, resistance, and opportunity. AI is no different. The key question is: Will today's executives repeat the mistakes of the past, or will they take bold steps to lead the AI revolution?

The lessons are clear—those who see AI's potential, embrace change, and act decisively will define the future. Those who don't? They'll be remembered like Blockbuster, Kodak, and the Luddites—businesses and leaders who failed to adapt and got left behind.

Chapter 3: From Uncertainty to Confidence – Developing an AI-Savvy Leadership Approach

In the face of rapid technological advancement, many executives find themselves at a crossroads—caught between the undeniable potential of artificial intelligence and the uncertainty of how to incorporate it into their strategic vision. AI is no longer a futuristic concept; it is an active force reshaping industries, altering competitive landscapes, and redefining how businesses operate. Yet, for many leaders, the complexity of AI, combined with its perceived risks, fuels hesitation. There is a lingering misconception that to lead an AI-driven organization, one must possess deep technical expertise, a belief that discourages many executives from taking proactive steps toward AI integration. However, history has repeatedly shown that successful leadership in times of disruption is not about mastering the underlying technology but about understanding its business implications and having the confidence to drive change. The transition from uncertainty to confidence in AI leadership is not just about acquiring knowledge—it is about developing a mindset that is adaptable, forward-thinking, and willing to embrace transformation.

The fear of AI is not new. Every major technological breakthrough has been met with skepticism and resistance. The Industrial Revolution faced opposition from those who believed mechanization would lead to mass unemployment. The internet was initially dismissed by many business leaders as a passing trend. Even the rise of digital transformation saw companies struggling to keep pace with evolving consumer expectations. Consider the case of Kodak, a company that once dominated the photography industry. Despite inventing the first digital camera, Kodak failed to fully embrace the technology, fearing it would cannibalize its film business. The result? Kodak lost its market relevance while digital-first competitors surged ahead. The lesson for today's executives is clear—waiting too long to adapt to disruptive innovation can have catastrophic consequences. AI is not a distant prospect; it is already driving efficiencies in industries from finance to healthcare, retail to manufacturing. The organizations that hesitate risk falling behind those that seize the moment and integrate AI into their strategic decision-making.

A fundamental shift in thinking is necessary for executives who aspire to be AI-savvy leaders. Many business leaders hold onto the notion that AI is purely a technical function—something to be handled by data scientists and IT departments. However, AI should not be confined to a silo; it is a strategic tool that affects every aspect of an organization, from customer engagement to operational efficiency, talent management to product innovation. Consider Satya Nadella's leadership at Microsoft. Despite not being an AI engineer, Nadella has transformed Microsoft into a global leader in AI-driven business solutions. His approach was not rooted in technical expertise but in a deep understanding of AI's transformative power. He championed a vision where AI was embedded into Microsoft's products, services, and culture, ensuring that every business function leveraged AI for competitive advantage. The most effective AI leaders are not those who write code but those who can bridge the gap between AI's capabilities and business strategy, identifying opportunities where AI can drive growth and efficiency.

One of the biggest barriers to AI adoption among executives is the fear of job displacement. Many leaders worry that AI will render large segments of their workforce obsolete, creating resistance to adoption. However, history suggests a different narrative — one where AI and automation enhance human capabilities rather than replace them entirely. When ATMs were introduced, many feared that bank tellers would become irrelevant. Instead, the opposite happened. Banks hired more tellers, not fewer, because ATMs allowed them to reallocate human resources to higher-value services, such as customer relationships and financial advising. A similar trend is emerging today. AI-powered tools are automating repetitive, mundane tasks, freeing up employees to focus on complex problem-solving, creativity, and strategic thinking. Forward-thinking executives recognize that AI is not a job destroyer but a job transformer. The key is not to resist automation but to rethink how human capital is deployed within an AI-augmented workplace. Companies that embrace this shift will gain a competitive advantage by unlocking new levels of productivity and innovation.

Another major misconception surrounding AI is that its implementation requires enormous financial investment, making it inaccessible to all but the largest corporations. However, the democratization of AI technologies has made them more accessible than ever before. Cloud-based AI solutions, machine learning-as-a-service platforms, and AI-powered analytics tools are readily available to businesses of all sizes. Companies no longer need to build AI infrastructure from scratch; they can leverage existing solutions to drive transformation. The success of Netflix serves as a powerful example of how AI-driven decision-making can revolutionize an industry. Through AI-powered content recommendations, Netflix has personalized the viewing experience for millions of subscribers, increasing engagement and customer retention. In contrast, Blockbuster, which failed to invest in AI-driven digital strategies, collapsed under the weight of outdated business models. The lesson is clear—AI is not a luxury for the elite few but a necessity for any organization that aims to remain competitive in a rapidly evolving business landscape.

For executives who feel overwhelmed by the complexity of AI, the path forward does not require an immediate, large-scale overhaul. The best AI leaders start with small, targeted initiatives that demonstrate AI's value before scaling up. The transition from uncertainty to confidence begins with a commitment to learning. Executives who immerse themselves in AI's fundamentals—reading industry reports, attending AI-focused conferences, engaging with AI experts—position themselves to make informed decisions. Surrounding oneself with a knowledgeable team is equally critical. AI adoption should not be the sole responsibility of IT departments; instead, cross-functional collaboration between business leaders, data scientists, and strategists ensures that AI initiatives align with broader organizational goals. Companies that foster an AI-first culture—one that encourages experimentation, data-driven decision-making, and continuous learning—create an environment where innovation thrives.

At its core, developing an AI-savvy leadership approach is not just about understanding AI technology but about embracing the mindset that AI represents an opportunity, not a threat. The transition from uncertainty to confidence requires a willingness to explore, experiment, and adapt. Executives who wait for AI to become a standardized, risk-free solution will find themselves left behind by those who take proactive steps today. The future of business will be shaped by leaders who recognize that AI is not a tool of the distant future but an essential force driving competitive advantage in the present.

PART 2: MASTERING AI-DRIVEN LEADERSHIP

Chapter 4: AI Demystified — What Every Executive Needs to Know

Artificial Intelligence has become one of the most overused buzzwords in modern business conversations. With every new product, service, or company claiming to be "AI-powered," executives often find themselves caught between excitement and skepticism. Some believe AI will single-handedly revolutionize industries, while others see it as an overhyped concept filled with exaggerated promises. The truth lies somewhere in between. AI is neither magic nor a passing trend—it is a powerful tool that, when understood and applied correctly, has the potential to transform businesses, drive efficiencies, and unlock new opportunities. For executives, mastering AI does not require a PhD in machine learning but rather a solid grasp of its practical applications, limitations, and strategic implications.

Understanding AI Without the Jargon

Many executives hesitate to engage deeply with AI because it often feels like a foreign language—filled with terms like neural networks, deep learning, natural language processing, and generative adversarial networks. While these technical concepts are important for data scientists, business leaders do not need to get lost in the complexity. At its core, AI is simply a system that enables machines to process information, recognize patterns, and make decisions with minimal human intervention.

One of the most common and accessible forms of AI is machine learning, where computers are trained on vast amounts of data to make predictions or classifications. For instance, when you shop on Amazon and receive personalized product recommendations, or when Netflix suggests a show based on your viewing history, these are examples of AI-driven machine learning models at work. Another major branch of AI is natural language processing (NLP), which allows machines to understand, interpret, and generate human language. Voice assistants like Siri and Alexa, as well as AI-powered chatbots used by customer service teams, rely on NLP to interact with users in a meaningful way.

A key distinction every executive must understand is the difference between narrow AI and general AI. Most AI applications today fall under narrow AI, meaning they are designed for specific tasks — such as detecting fraud in banking, predicting equipment failures in manufacturing, or optimizing marketing campaigns. General AI, which would possess human-like reasoning and adaptability across a wide range of tasks, remains largely theoretical and is not something businesses will be integrating anytime soon. Recognizing this distinction helps executives focus on the real-world applications of AI rather than getting distracted by futuristic speculation.

Cutting Through the Hype: What AI Can and Cannot Do

The widespread excitement around AI has led to grand claims about its capabilities, but not all of them are grounded in reality. Executives must be able to separate practical AI solutions from overinflated marketing promises.

A prime example of AI hype was IBM's Watson, which famously won Jeopardy! in 2011 and was later marketed as a revolutionary tool for diagnosing diseases and transforming healthcare. While Watson did achieve impressive feats in natural language processing, it struggled in real-world medical applications, where incomplete data and complex human decision-making made it less effective than expected. The lesson here is clear—just because an AI system can excel in a controlled environment does not mean it will seamlessly translate into every industry.

On the other hand, there are areas where AI has genuinely delivered remarkable results. In financial services, AI-driven fraud detection systems analyze millions of transactions in real time, identifying suspicious patterns that human analysts might miss. In supply chain management, AI-powered demand forecasting tools help companies optimize inventory levels, reducing waste and improving efficiency. In healthcare, AI algorithms assist radiologists in detecting tumors in medical images with greater accuracy than traditional methods. These are practical, proven use cases where AI is already driving significant business value.

However, AI is not a one-size-fits-all solution. It struggles with tasks that require deep common sense, ethical judgment, or emotional intelligence. For example, while AI can generate human-like text or analyze historical data to make predictions, it cannot replace the intuition, creativity, and ethical reasoning that great leaders bring to decision-making. This means that while AI can enhance executive capabilities, it should be seen as a co-pilot rather than a replacement for human leadership.

How Executives Can Build AI Competency Without Becoming Technologists

One of the biggest misconceptions about AI is that mastering it requires deep technical expertise. In reality, executives do not need to become data scientists—they need to develop AI fluency, which means understanding the strategic and operational implications of AI rather than the intricate technical details.

A prime example of AI-savvy leadership is Sundar Pichai, CEO of Google. While he is not an AI researcher by background, he has successfully steered Google into becoming an AI-first company by prioritizing investments in machine learning, cloud-based AI services, and AI-powered products like Google Search and Google Assistant. His leadership demonstrates that an executive's role is not to build AI models but to identify where AI can create business value, align it with company strategy, and build teams that can execute AI initiatives effectively.

For executives looking to enhance their AI competency, the first step is immersing themselves in real-world AI use cases. Reading AI reports from McKinsey, Gartner, or MIT Sloan can provide valuable insights into how businesses are leveraging AI across different industries. Attending AI-focused conferences and engaging with AI experts can also help leaders stay ahead of trends and emerging technologies.

Another critical step is creating a culture of AI experimentation within their organizations. Instead of waiting for a "perfect" AI strategy, forward-thinking executives launch small, low-risk AI pilot projects to test the technology's impact before scaling up. Companies like Procter & Gamble and Unilever have successfully used this approach by implementing AI in targeted areas such as demand forecasting, personalized marketing, and supply chain optimization before expanding AI adoption across the enterprise.

Additionally, executives must ensure that their organizations have the right AI talent and partnerships. Rather than trying to build everything in-house, many successful companies collaborate with AI startups, cloud providers like AWS and Microsoft Azure, or academic institutions to accelerate AI adoption. For instance, BMW has partnered with AI firms to optimize its manufacturing processes, while JPMorgan Chase has leveraged AI-powered legal contract analysis tools to improve efficiency in its legal operations.

The Executive's Role in an AI-Driven Future

Ultimately, the most effective AI-driven executives are those who embrace AI as a strategic enabler rather than a threat or an obligation. They recognize that AI is not about replacing human decision-making but about enhancing it with better data, faster insights, and automated efficiencies. They lead by example—championing AI literacy, fostering a culture of innovation, and ensuring that AI aligns with the company's mission and values.

AI is not something executives can afford to ignore or delegate entirely to technical teams. Just as digital transformation reshaped the role of leadership in the past decade, AI is now doing the same. The organizations that thrive in this new era will be those led by AI-savvy executives who can cut through the noise, identify real opportunities, and drive AI-powered innovation with confidence.

Chapter 5: The AI Playbook – Five Business-Critical AI Applications You Must Leverage

Artificial Intelligence is no longer a futuristic concept—it is a present-day competitive advantage. Organizations that fail to integrate AI into their business models risk falling behind as AI-driven companies optimize operations, enhance customer experiences, and develop innovative products at an unprecedented pace. However, executives often struggle with the practical side of AI adoption. The key to success is not chasing the latest AI trends but focusing on proven, business-critical AI applications that drive measurable value.

AI is not a monolithic technology but a set of tools that can be applied in various business contexts. While some companies experiment with AI for the sake of appearing innovative, the most successful leaders implement AI strategically, aligning it with their core business goals. This chapter explores five essential AI applications that executives must leverage to gain a competitive edge, increase efficiency, and drive innovation.

AI in Customer Experience: The Shift from Transactions to Intelligent Engagement

One of the most visible and impactful uses of AI is in customer experience (CX). Businesses are moving away from transactional customer interactions and toward AI-driven, personalized engagement. Companies like Amazon, Netflix, and Starbucks have set the gold standard for AI-powered personalization, using data to anticipate customer preferences and tailor recommendations.

For instance, Netflix's AI-driven recommendation engine analyzes a user's watch history, viewing time, and even the time of day they watch to suggest content that keeps them engaged. Similarly, Starbucks' AI-powered loyalty program uses customer data to provide personalized offers and predict purchasing behavior, increasing revenue and customer retention.

Chatbots and AI-powered virtual assistants are also revolutionizing customer service. Instead of waiting on hold for human representatives, customers can now interact with AI-driven chatbots that resolve issues in real time. Bank of America's Erica, an AI-powered virtual financial assistant, helps customers check balances, schedule payments, and even provide financial insights based on their spending habits. These AI systems are not just cost-saving measures but are also enhancing customer satisfaction by providing instant, personalized, and seamless experiences.

AI in Operations and Process Automation: The Path to Unmatched Efficiency

AI is redefining business operations by eliminating inefficiencies and automating repetitive tasks. Intelligent automation, powered by robotic process automation (RPA) and AI-driven decision-making, is helping companies reduce costs and improve accuracy.

For example, AI-powered automation is transforming finance departments. JPMorgan Chase uses AI to analyze legal documents, reducing the time it takes to review contracts from 360,000 hours annually to mere seconds. In healthcare, AI-driven scheduling tools optimize patient appointments and hospital resource allocation, ensuring maximum efficiency and reduced wait times.

Manufacturing is another sector seeing tremendous gains from AI-driven automation. Siemens and General Electric use AI-powered predictive maintenance, analyzing sensor data to detect potential equipment failures before they happen. This not only prevents costly downtimes but also extends the lifespan of critical machinery.

AI is also making supply chains more resilient. Walmart and Amazon use AI-driven demand forecasting, predicting inventory needs with high precision to ensure shelves are always stocked without unnecessary waste. The ability to make data-driven supply chain decisions allows businesses to respond to market fluctuations faster and more effectively than ever before.

AI in Decision-Making: Augmenting Human Intelligence with Data-Driven Insights

AI is no longer just about automation—it is also about augmenting human decision-making with insights that would be impossible for humans to analyze manually. The volume of data generated in today's business landscape is overwhelming, but AI can process and interpret this data in real time, turning it into actionable intelligence.

Take the financial industry as an example. AI-powered algorithmic trading systems, used by firms like Goldman Sachs and BlackRock, analyze millions of data points per second, detecting market trends and executing trades faster than any human could. In marketing, AI-powered tools analyze customer sentiment from social media, reviews, and surveys to help brands refine messaging and product offerings based on real-time consumer feedback.

AI-driven HR analytics is also changing how companies recruit and manage talent. AI can analyze resumes, predict employee performance, and even detect patterns that indicate burnout or dissatisfaction, allowing HR teams to take proactive measures. Companies like Unilever have adopted AI-driven hiring tools to screen job applicants, using AI-powered video analysis to assess candidates' facial expressions, tone, and language patterns to predict cultural fit.

AI in Product and Service Innovation: Creating the Next-Generation Offerings

AI is not just improving existing processes — it is also enabling the development of entirely new products and services. AI-powered innovation is at the core of many tech giants' strategies, but it is also transforming traditional industries.

Consider how Tesla has redefined the automotive industry with AI-driven self-driving technology. By continuously collecting and analyzing data from millions of vehicles, Tesla's AI learns and improves over time, making autonomous driving safer and more reliable. Similarly, Spotify's AI-driven music discovery algorithms ensure that users discover new songs tailored to their tastes, enhancing user engagement and satisfaction.

Beyond consumer products, AI is also driving drug discovery and personalized medicine. Pharmaceutical companies like Pfizer and Moderna use AI to accelerate drug development, helping them analyze vast datasets to identify potential compounds for new treatments. AI-driven gene sequencing and precision medicine are allowing doctors to create personalized treatment plans based on an individual's genetic makeup, revolutionizing healthcare.

AI in Risk Management and Cybersecurity: The First Line of Defense Against Threats

As businesses become more digitally interconnected, the risk of cyber threats increases. AI has become an essential tool in detecting, preventing, and mitigating cybersecurity risks. AI-driven cybersecurity solutions analyze network traffic, detect anomalies, and identify potential cyberattacks before they cause damage.

For example, financial institutions use AI-driven fraud detection systems to monitor millions of transactions in real time, flagging suspicious activity. Mastercard's AI fraud detection system identifies anomalies in purchasing behavior, preventing fraudulent transactions before they occur. Similarly, IBM's Watson for Cybersecurity scans vast amounts of threat intelligence data, helping organizations anticipate and respond to security threats.

AI is also improving compliance and regulatory monitoring. Banks and insurance companies leverage AI to analyze transactions and ensure compliance with regulations, reducing the risk of penalties and legal issues. By automating compliance monitoring, AI helps companies stay ahead of regulatory changes while minimizing operational risks.

The Future of AI-Driven Business Strategy

For executives, leveraging AI is no longer optional — it is a strategic imperative. Those who understand how to integrate AI across customer experience, operations, decision-making, innovation, and risk management will position their organizations for sustained success. However, AI adoption is not just about deploying new technologies; it requires a cultural shift — one where leaders foster AI literacy, encourage experimentation, and align AI strategies with long-term business goals.

The most successful AI-driven leaders recognize that AI is not here to replace them but to enhance their decision-making, automate repetitive tasks, and unlock new opportunities. The businesses that thrive in the AI era will not be the ones that fear disruption but the ones that embrace AI as a core driver of growth, efficiency, and innovation.

Chapter 6: The Leadership Dilemma – How AI Helps Avoid Bias and Improve Decision-Making

Leadership has always been about making informed, strategic decisions that drive organizations forward. However, decision-making is rarely as objective as leaders might believe. Cognitive biases, organizational politics, and incomplete information often cloud judgment, leading to inefficiencies, missed opportunities, and even ethical missteps. In today's rapidly evolving business landscape, where executives must navigate complex, high-stakes decisions, AI has emerged as a powerful tool to enhance decision-making, minimize bias, and ensure better outcomes.

Artificial Intelligence does not suffer from human emotions, preconceived notions, or unconscious prejudices. It processes vast amounts of data objectively, recognizes patterns humans might miss, and offers insights based on logic rather than intuition. Yet, AI is not a magic solution. It must be implemented thoughtfully to avoid reinforcing existing biases and ensure that decision-making remains transparent, ethical, and aligned with organizational goals. In this chapter, we explore how AI helps executives overcome bias, enhance decision-making, and cultivate a more data-driven leadership approach.

Understanding Bias in Leadership Decisions

Cognitive biases are hardwired into human decision-making. Even the most seasoned executives fall prey to confirmation bias (seeking information that supports pre-existing beliefs), availability bias (relying on immediate examples rather than broader data), and anchoring bias (giving undue weight to initial information). These biases can lead to poor strategic choices, hiring mistakes, and flawed risk assessments.

Consider the case of Kodak, once a dominant force in the photography industry. Despite having access to digital camera technology as early as the 1970s, Kodak's leadership dismissed it, believing film would remain the preferred medium. Their confirmation bias—clinging to the idea that their existing business model would endure—blinded them to digital disruption, leading to their eventual downfall.

Similarly, hiring decisions are often plagued by unconscious bias. Studies have shown that hiring managers tend to favor candidates with backgrounds, interests, or demographics similar to their own, leading to a lack of diversity and innovation. AI-powered resume screening tools are helping organizations mitigate these biases by focusing on skills and qualifications rather than subjective factors. Companies like Unilever and Hilton have successfully implemented AI-driven recruitment systems, reducing bias while improving efficiency.

How AI Enhances Decision-Making with Data-Driven Insights

AI's greatest strength in leadership decision-making lies in its ability to process and analyze vast amounts of data without bias. Unlike humans, AI does not rely on intuition or gut feelings; it identifies trends, patterns, and correlations that are often imperceptible to human decision-makers.

Take the financial industry, for example. AI-powered trading algorithms used by firms like Goldman Sachs and JPMorgan Chase analyze millions of data points per second, making split-second trading decisions based on objective criteria rather than human emotions like fear or greed. This data-driven approach has not only increased profitability but also minimized risks associated with impulsive decision-making.

AI is also transforming corporate strategy and market analysis. Instead of relying solely on traditional market research, executives now use AI-driven analytics to understand consumer behavior, predict trends, and anticipate shifts in demand. Retail giants like Walmart and Target use AI-powered demand forecasting to optimize inventory, ensuring they stock the right products at the right time. This approach eliminates guesswork, reducing waste and increasing efficiency.

In healthcare, AI-driven diagnostics have demonstrated higher accuracy rates than human doctors in detecting diseases like cancer. IBM Watson Health, for instance, analyzes patient records, medical journals, and clinical trials to recommend treatment plans that are data-backed rather than influenced by a doctor's individual experience or biases. This augments medical decision-making, ensuring better patient outcomes.

Avoiding the Pitfalls: When AI Inherits Human Bias

While AI holds immense potential to reduce bias, it is not immune to it. AI systems are only as objective as the data they are trained on. If an AI model is trained on biased historical data, it can perpetuate or even amplify existing biases rather than eliminate them.

A well-documented case is that of AI-powered hiring algorithms used by Amazon, which unintentionally favored male candidates because they were trained on past hiring data that reflected a male-dominated workforce. Since the AI learned from biased patterns, it deprioritized resumes with words like "women's leadership club" or "women's soccer team," reinforcing existing gender disparities. Amazon eventually scrapped the system, highlighting the importance of ethical AI implementation.

To prevent such biases, organizations must implement continuous auditing, transparency, and human oversight when deploying AI for decision-making. AI models should be regularly tested for fairness, with diverse teams ensuring that training data reflects a broad, representative sample. Google's AI ethics team and Microsoft's AI Fairness initiative are leading examples of how companies are proactively addressing AI bias and ensuring responsible AI deployment.

AI and the Future of Leadership Decision-Making

AI is not here to replace human judgment but to enhance and support it. The best executives are not those who blindly follow AI's recommendations but those who use AI as a collaborative tool, combining its analytical power with their strategic thinking, experience, and ethical considerations.

The organizations that thrive in the AI era will be the ones that embrace AI-driven decision-making while ensuring that human oversight, ethical considerations, and diverse perspectives remain integral to the process. Leadership in the age of AI is not about surrendering decision-making to machines but about leveraging AI to make more informed, fair, and strategic choices.

As AI continues to evolve, the most successful leaders will be those who recognize that true intelligence lies in the fusion of human judgment and machine-driven insights, creating a future where decisions are more data-driven, less biased, and ultimately more effective.

Chapter 7: From Data to Action – Accelerating Insight–Driven Decision Making

In the modern business landscape, data is the new currency — but raw data alone is not enough. Organizations generate vast amounts of information daily, yet many leaders struggle to translate this data into actionable insights that drive business success. The challenge is not in collecting data but in extracting meaningful patterns, making timely decisions, and turning insights into concrete strategies.

AI-powered decision-making is revolutionizing how executives harness data for real-time, high-impact choices. By leveraging machine learning, predictive analytics, and automation, businesses can move beyond traditional gut-feeling decision-making and enter an era where every strategic move is backed by intelligent, data-driven insights. However, simply having access to AI-driven analytics does not guarantee success — leaders must know how to interpret, trust, and act on AI-generated recommendations.

This chapter explores how executives can accelerate insight-driven decision-making, transform data into action, and create a culture where AI-powered intelligence becomes a fundamental pillar of leadership.

The Data Dilemma: Why Information Alone Is Not Enough

Every company, regardless of industry, is now a data company. Retailers analyze consumer purchases, hospitals track patient outcomes, manufacturers monitor supply chains, and financial institutions assess risks — all through vast streams of data. Yet, despite this abundance, many businesses fail to capitalize on their data's full potential.

A striking example comes from the early days of Nokia, once the world's dominant mobile phone manufacturer. The company had access to data showing shifting consumer preferences toward touchscreen devices. However, instead of acting on this insight, Nokia's leadership dismissed the trend, believing their existing keypad models would continue to dominate the market. The failure to transform data into action allowed competitors like Apple and Samsung to capitalize on the touchscreen revolution, leaving Nokia struggling to regain relevance.

A more successful case is Netflix, which has mastered the art of data-driven decision-making. Using AI-driven recommendation engines, Netflix analyzes viewer habits, predicts preferences, and tailors content accordingly. When producing original series like House of Cards, Netflix didn't just rely on creative intuition — it used data insights to determine which actors, directors, and storytelling elements would most likely engage audiences. This strategic use of AI-powered analytics propelled Netflix into becoming a global entertainment powerhouse.

AI as the Catalyst for Smarter, Faster Decision-Making

AI is not just about analyzing historical data; its true power lies in its ability to predict, recommend, and automate decision-making in real time. Companies that integrate AI into their decision-making processes gain a significant competitive advantage by acting faster and more precisely than their rivals.

One of the best examples is Amazon's supply chain optimization. The company uses AI-driven forecasting models to anticipate demand fluctuations and adjust inventory levels dynamically. Instead of relying on traditional logistics planning, which is often reactive, Amazon's AI systems predict what customers will need before they even place an order, ensuring products are stocked in the right warehouses and shipped with minimal delays. This insight-driven approach has given Amazon an unparalleled edge in e-commerce logistics, allowing it to offer one-day or even same-day deliveries.

Similarly, AI-driven fraud detection systems in financial services help banks like JPMorgan Chase and HSBC prevent fraudulent transactions in real time. Instead of manually reviewing suspicious activity, AI continuously monitors transaction patterns, flags anomalies, and blocks fraudulent activities before financial damage occurs. These systems accelerate decision-making while reducing human error, ensuring a more secure financial ecosystem.

Bridging the Gap: Turning AI-Generated Insights into Leadership Action

For AI-driven decision-making to be truly transformative, leaders must trust AI insights and integrate them into their strategic processes. However, a significant challenge remains—many executives, particularly those with traditional leadership backgrounds, struggle to move beyond intuition-based decision-making.

This hesitation was evident in General Motors' (GM) approach to electric vehicles (EVs). For years, despite mounting data on consumer demand for sustainable transportation, GM hesitated to shift its focus from gas-powered vehicles. Meanwhile, Tesla, guided by data-backed projections on battery efficiency and market potential, aggressively expanded its EV production, leaving GM scrambling to catch up.

Successful AI-driven leadership requires a blend of trust in technology and human oversight. A prime example is Johnson & Johnson's use of AI in drug development. The pharmaceutical giant uses AI to analyze billions of medical records and genetic data to identify potential new drug formulations. However, instead of blindly accepting AI's recommendations, human researchers validate, test, and refine AI-generated insights, ensuring scientific rigor while accelerating innovation.

Building an AI-First Leadership Culture

To fully embrace AI-driven decision-making, organizations must cultivate a culture where data is at the core of leadership. This requires:

- AI Literacy at the Executive Level – Leaders must understand AI's capabilities and limitations to make informed decisions. Companies like Google and Microsoft actively train their executives on AI principles, ensuring that leadership decisions are aligned with technological advancements.

- Collaboration Between AI and Human Expertise – AI should be seen as a co-pilot rather than a replacement for human decision-making. The most successful AI-driven companies use AI for data analysis but rely on human judgment for ethical, strategic, and creative insights.

- Agility in Acting on Insights – Organizations that leverage AI must act quickly. The difference between market leaders and laggards often lies in how fast they turn AI insights into concrete business strategies.

In today's business world, data alone is not power — actionable insights and rapid execution are the real competitive advantages. The companies and leaders who embrace AI-powered decision-making will be the ones who drive innovation, outpace competitors, and redefine industry standards in the digital age.

Chapter 8: Balancing Today and Tomorrow – Navigating AI's Short–Term and Long–Term Impact

AI is reshaping industries at an unprecedented pace, forcing executives to strike a delicate balance between short-term implementation and long-term transformation. Many leaders find themselves caught between two competing pressures—delivering immediate business results using AI while simultaneously preparing for the radical shifts AI will bring in the coming decades. This tension is not new; history has repeatedly shown how technological revolutions challenge traditional business models, leaving behind those who fail to anticipate the future.

The challenge for executives is not just about adopting AI—it's about making strategic decisions that ensure both present stability and future competitiveness. Those who focus solely on short-term AI applications risk missing the deeper structural shifts that AI will bring, while those who concentrate only on the distant future may fail to realize the immediate business gains AI offers today.

This chapter explores how AI-driven leaders can effectively navigate AI's short-term and long-term impact, ensuring that today's AI strategies align with the broader, future-driven vision of their organizations.

The Short-Term AI Imperative: Delivering Immediate Business Impact

Executives are under constant pressure to demonstrate quick wins with AI adoption. Shareholders, customers, and internal stakeholders expect tangible results — whether in cost reductions, efficiency improvements, or enhanced customer experiences. Organizations that successfully integrate AI into their short-term operations gain an immediate edge over their competitors, but short-term success should not come at the expense of long-term vision.

A perfect example is McDonald's use of AI-powered automation in its drive-thru operations. The company recently deployed AI-driven voice assistants and predictive ordering technology to speed up service times and improve customer personalization. By analyzing vast amounts of real-time order data, McDonald's AI systems anticipate customer preferences and optimize menu suggestions, leading to increased order values and faster transactions. This short-term AI implementation has generated immediate revenue gains and operational efficiencies without requiring a fundamental shift in McDonald's business model.

Similarly, financial institutions are leveraging AI for fraud detection and risk assessment. Banks like HSBC and JPMorgan Chase have integrated AI-driven algorithms that analyze real-time transaction patterns, detect anomalies, and prevent fraudulent activities within seconds. These implementations deliver instant security enhancements, protecting both customers and financial institutions from losses.

However, companies that only focus on AI's short-term impact without aligning it with a broader strategy risk missing the bigger picture. AI is not just about automating tasks or cutting costs — it is about reshaping industries, business models, and customer expectations for the long term.

The Long-Term AI Imperative: Reshaping Industries and Workforce Dynamics

While short-term AI gains are essential, long-term AI transformation is inevitable. The way businesses operate today will be fundamentally different in the next decade due to advancements in generative AI, autonomous systems, and AI-driven decision-making. Leaders who fail to plan for this future risk obsolescence, much like Blockbuster failed to anticipate the rise of streaming services while Netflix invested in AI-driven content personalization and digital distribution.

A compelling example of long-term AI transformation is Tesla's vision for fully autonomous vehicles. Unlike traditional automakers that focus on incremental improvements in driver assistance technologies, Tesla has built its AI strategy around a future where human drivers will no longer be necessary. By continuously training its AI models through billions of real-world driving miles, Tesla is not just improving short-term performance — it is shaping the future of mobility itself.

In the healthcare sector, companies like DeepMind and IBM Watson Health are investing in AI-powered drug discovery and predictive diagnostics. These initiatives will not generate immediate profits but will revolutionize the medical field in the coming decades. By using AI to analyze genetic data, detect diseases earlier, and personalize treatment plans, the long-term implications for patient care and medical research are profound.

However, long-term AI adoption also raises critical ethical, regulatory, and workforce challenges. The transition to AI-driven industries will inevitably lead to job displacement, shifts in workforce skill requirements, and new regulatory considerations. AI-savvy executives must proactively address these challenges by investing in employee retraining programs, advocating for ethical AI use, and engaging policymakers to ensure responsible AI governance.

Bridging the Gap: Creating an AI Strategy That Balances Today and Tomorrow

One of the biggest mistakes executives make is treating short-term AI applications and long-term AI transformation as separate initiatives. Instead, the most successful organizations integrate AI into a cohesive strategy that delivers immediate value while preparing for long-term shifts.

Take Amazon's approach to AI investment as an example. In the short term, Amazon has used AI to enhance its supply chain logistics, personalized recommendations, and fraud prevention — all of which provide direct, measurable benefits to the company's bottom line. Simultaneously, Amazon is making long-term AI bets on autonomous delivery through drones, AI-powered customer service chatbots, and even AI-driven cashier-less stores. These initiatives might not yield immediate returns, but they position Amazon for sustained dominance in the retail and logistics industries over the next decade.

Executives must ask themselves:

- Are we leveraging AI today in a way that generates immediate value while positioning us for the future?

- Are we making strategic AI investments that go beyond automation and cost-cutting, and instead reshape our industry?

- How are we preparing our workforce for the inevitable AI-driven shifts in skills and job roles?

A well-balanced AI strategy requires leadership vision, adaptability, and a willingness to embrace both incremental and disruptive change. Organizations that fail to bridge the gap between AI's short-term benefits and long-term transformation risk becoming irrelevant in an AI-driven world.

The companies and leaders that will thrive in the AI era are not just those who implement AI today—but those who shape the future with it.

Chapter 9: AI as Your Strategic Advantage – Faster, Smarter, and More Agile Leadership

The modern executive landscape is evolving at an extraordinary pace, with AI at the heart of this transformation. Leaders who fail to recognize AI as a strategic advantage will struggle to compete against those who embrace it as a force multiplier for agility, intelligence, and decision-making. The most successful businesses today are not simply using AI as a tool—they are integrating it into their leadership philosophy, redefining how they approach strategy, operations, and customer engagement.

AI is more than just an automation engine; it is a cognitive extension of leadership, enabling executives to move faster, make smarter decisions, and respond to market shifts with unprecedented agility. In a world where change is constant, AI-driven leaders have an edge: they anticipate trends before they happen, mitigate risks before they escalate, and capitalize on opportunities before their competitors even recognize them.

AI and Speed: Outpacing the Competition in Real-Time Decision-Making

In today's hyper-competitive business environment, speed is a defining factor of success. Organizations that make faster, data-driven decisions consistently outperform their slower-moving rivals. Traditional decision-making processes rely heavily on human intuition, past experiences, and often bureaucratic hierarchies, which slow down critical responses to market disruptions. AI, however, eliminates these inefficiencies by analyzing vast amounts of data in real time and presenting leaders with actionable insights instantly.

Consider Goldman Sachs' AI-driven trading algorithms. The company has replaced large portions of its human trading floor with machine-learning models that analyze global financial data in milliseconds, making real-time trading decisions that no human could match. By leveraging AI, Goldman Sachs executes thousands of trades per second, capitalizing on fleeting opportunities that manual traders would miss. This ability to process, analyze, and act on data at an accelerated pace gives AI-driven firms a competitive edge.

Retail giants like Zara also demonstrate the power of AI in supply chain agility. Unlike traditional fashion retailers that operate on seasonal collections, Zara leverages AI to analyze customer preferences, social media trends, and in-store data to modify its designs in real time. As a result, the company releases new fashion lines within weeks, not months, outpacing competitors who rely on outdated trend predictions. AI enables Zara to adapt quickly to consumer demand, optimize inventory, and reduce waste, proving that agility is as much about survival as it is about success.

AI is not just about making businesses faster; it is about making leaders more responsive, adaptive, and decisive. In industries where timing can mean the difference between domination and disruption, AI-driven executives operate at a higher level of speed and efficiency, ensuring their organizations remain ahead of the curve.

AI and Intelligence: Smarter Decision-Making with Enhanced Predictive Capabilities

A major misconception about AI is that it replaces human judgment. In reality, AI enhances human intelligence, providing leaders with unparalleled predictive insights that lead to better strategic choices. AI-driven analytics allow executives to see patterns in complex datasets, forecast market trends, and identify risks before they become critical issues.

The healthcare industry provides a compelling case study. Mayo Clinic and IBM Watson Health have integrated AI into their diagnostic systems to predict diseases before they manifest. AI-driven models analyze millions of patient records, genetic sequences, and environmental factors to identify potential health risks long before symptoms appear. For executives in healthcare, AI is not just a tool—it is a life-saving asset that improves patient outcomes and revolutionizes medical research.

In the business world, AI-driven consumer analytics have transformed customer engagement. Companies like Netflix and Spotify use AI-powered recommendation engines to predict user preferences with astonishing accuracy. These algorithms analyze millions of data points on user behavior, past interactions, and real-time engagement to deliver personalized content that increases customer retention and satisfaction. By understanding what consumers want before they even realize it themselves, AI-driven companies gain a strategic advantage in customer loyalty and brand differentiation.

For executives, AI-driven intelligence eliminates guesswork. It ensures that business decisions are based on data-driven insights rather than instinct, reducing risks and maximizing outcomes. AI is not a replacement for strategic thinking—it is an enhancement of it, empowering leaders to make informed choices that drive sustainable growth and innovation.

AI and Agility: Transforming Leadership in an Era of Constant Change

The ability to pivot and adapt is a defining trait of successful leadership. However, traditional business models often suffer from rigid structures, slow approval processes, and resistance to change. AI changes this paradigm by enabling organizations to become more agile, experiment rapidly, and innovate without hesitation.

One of the best examples of AI-driven agility is Tesla's approach to vehicle software updates. Unlike traditional automakers that require costly recalls for performance enhancements, Tesla uses AI-powered over-the-air (OTA) updates to continuously improve its vehicles. AI-driven data analysis from Tesla's fleet allows the company to refine autopilot features, enhance battery efficiency, and fix potential issues remotely—all without requiring customers to visit a service center. This level of adaptability sets Tesla apart from competitors stuck in legacy production cycles.

Similarly, Unilever leverages AI in its supply chain management to maintain agility in global operations. The company uses machine learning algorithms to analyze raw material availability, geopolitical risks, and shifting consumer preferences, allowing it to adjust manufacturing outputs in real time. This AI-driven adaptability ensures that Unilever remains resilient in the face of global disruptions, from economic downturns to supply chain bottlenecks.

Executives who fail to incorporate AI into their leadership approach risk becoming obsolete in industries that demand constant reinvention. Agility is no longer a luxury—it is a necessity. AI-powered leaders embrace change, anticipate shifts, and use AI insights to guide their organizations toward long-term success.

The AI-Driven Leader's Competitive Edge

AI is not just a technological upgrade—it is a leadership transformation tool. The executives who thrive in the AI era are those who understand that speed, intelligence, and agility are no longer optional—they are business imperatives. Whether it's making rapid decisions, leveraging predictive insights, or maintaining adaptability in uncertain markets, AI is the differentiator between companies that lead and those that follow.

Organizations that treat AI as a strategic advantage rather than a mere operational tool will outpace their competitors, drive innovation, and redefine their industries. The AI-driven leader is not just a participant in digital transformation—they are the architect of it.

PART 3: BUILDING AN AI-SAVVY ORGANIZATI ON

Chapter 10: Leading with Vision – Aligning AI Initiatives with Business Strategy

AI is no longer an experimental technology—it is a fundamental driver of business strategy. The organizations that successfully leverage AI do not treat it as a standalone project but as an integrated pillar of their vision and long-term objectives. The challenge, however, is that many executives struggle to align AI initiatives with broader business goals. Too often, AI is implemented in isolated departments or as a reactive measure to keep up with industry trends rather than as a proactive enabler of strategic transformation.

To lead with vision, executives must bridge the gap between AI's technical capabilities and its business value, ensuring that AI investments drive measurable growth, innovation, and competitive differentiation. Companies that succeed in this endeavor do not merely adopt AI—they embed it into their decision-making, customer engagement, and operational efficiency strategies.

AI as a Strategic Enabler, Not Just a Tool

Executives often make the mistake of viewing AI as a technology problem rather than a business opportunity. They invest in AI solutions without a clear business case, leading to disjointed projects that fail to deliver long-term value. A visionary leader, however, sees AI as an enabler of organizational transformation, aligning it with financial goals, market positioning, and customer experience strategies.

Take Amazon, for example. Rather than adopting AI as a series of disconnected initiatives, Amazon has woven AI into the fabric of its entire business model. From AI-driven supply chain optimization and personalized recommendations to voice assistants like Alexa, Amazon treats AI as a core strategic asset rather than an experimental add-on. The result? Enhanced efficiency, superior customer experiences, and a dominant market position that competitors struggle to replicate.

Similarly, JPMorgan Chase has embedded AI into its risk management and fraud detection frameworks. By integrating AI-driven predictive analytics into its financial strategies, the bank anticipates potential economic downturns, detects fraudulent transactions in real-time, and automates investment strategies for clients. Instead of treating AI as a back-office function, JPMorgan Chase has aligned it with its business model, ensuring that AI contributes directly to profitability, security, and customer trust.

Executives must ask themselves: Is AI supporting my company's strategic goals, or is it just another tech project? Without a clear answer to this question, AI investments risk becoming inefficient, costly, and directionless.

The Role of AI in Competitive Differentiation

One of AI's most significant advantages is its ability to differentiate companies in crowded markets. Businesses that harness AI effectively gain a first-mover advantage, creating new value propositions that competitors struggle to match. AI-driven organizations do not just react to market trends—they define them.

Consider Tesla's AI-powered self-driving technology. While traditional automakers focused on refining internal combustion engines, Tesla rewrote the rules of competition by integrating AI into autonomous driving capabilities. The company's AI-driven neural networks process billions of miles of real-world driving data, allowing Tesla to improve its autopilot system faster than regulatory bodies can legislate. By embedding AI into its strategic roadmap, Tesla has transformed itself from an automaker into a technology-driven mobility leader.

Similarly, Airbnb uses AI to personalize travel experiences, leveraging machine learning to recommend tailored lodging options based on user preferences, past searches, and behavioral data. This AI-driven personalization allows Airbnb to compete against traditional hotel chains, offering guests a uniquely tailored experience that hotels with rigid pricing models and standardized services cannot replicate.

For AI-driven leaders, the lesson is clear: AI should not merely enhance existing processes—it should create entirely new competitive advantages. Executives must think beyond automation and efficiency gains, asking, How can AI redefine our industry? How can it make us indispensable to our customers? Those who answer these questions with bold, AI-powered strategies will not just survive the digital era—they will dominate it.

Creating an AI Roadmap for Sustainable Growth

For AI to deliver long-term value, organizations need a clear AI roadmap—one that aligns with business priorities and evolves alongside technological advancements. Many companies rush into AI investments without considering scalability, integration, or long-term sustainability, leading to short-lived successes that fail to generate lasting impact.

Executives should focus on three key pillars when developing an AI roadmap:

1. Defining Business Objectives – AI initiatives should be mapped directly to organizational goals, whether it's increasing revenue, improving customer retention, reducing operational costs, or enhancing innovation. Every AI investment should answer the question: How does this contribute to our long-term success?

2. Building Cross-Functional AI Teams – AI adoption cannot be limited to IT departments. Successful implementation requires collaboration between data scientists, business strategists, marketing teams, and operations executives. A siloed approach will only lead to fragmented AI deployments that fail to scale.

3. Investing in AI Governance and Ethics – As AI becomes more integral to business operations, ethical considerations must be a priority. Issues such as bias in AI decision-making, data privacy concerns, and regulatory compliance need to be addressed proactively. Visionary leaders recognize that responsible AI adoption is not just a legal necessity—it is a competitive advantage in a world where trust and transparency drive consumer loyalty.

AI is no longer an experimental playground for tech enthusiasts—it is the foundation of 21st-century business strategy. The companies that thrive in the AI era are those led by executives who recognize AI's transformative potential and align it with their strategic vision. AI-driven leadership is not just about adopting new technologies—it is about reshaping industries, redefining competition, and reimagining what is possible in the digital economy.

Chapter 11: The First 90 Days – How Executives Can Implement AI for Immediate Impact

The first 90 days of any leadership initiative are critical, and AI adoption is no different. For executives stepping into AI-driven transformation, the challenge is not only understanding AI's potential but also turning that understanding into action—fast. While AI adoption can feel like an overwhelming, long-term journey, successful leaders recognize that meaningful impact can be achieved within the first three months. The key lies in setting the right priorities, aligning stakeholders, and establishing quick wins that build momentum.

AI Adoption Begins with a Leadership Mindset Shift

One of the biggest hurdles in AI implementation is not the technology itself but the mindset surrounding it. Many organizations see AI as a complex, futuristic concept rather than a practical business tool that can drive immediate efficiency, revenue, and customer satisfaction. The first step for executives is to demystify AI for their teams, shifting the conversation from vague possibilities to tangible, results-driven strategies.

Take Satya Nadella's leadership at Microsoft as an example. When he took over as CEO, Microsoft was lagging behind in cloud computing and AI adoption. Rather than treating AI as a technical challenge, Nadella repositioned it as a core business driver, embedding AI into Microsoft's products and services, from Office 365's AI-powered productivity tools to Azure's AI cloud services. This mindset shift allowed Microsoft to rapidly scale AI initiatives, making AI a fundamental part of the company's growth strategy within his first year of leadership.

For any executive, the first 90 days should be focused on embedding AI into the organization's DNA, ensuring that leadership teams, employees, and stakeholders understand that AI is not a passing trend but an essential business enabler. Without this cultural shift, even the most sophisticated AI strategies will fail to gain traction.

Identifying Quick Wins: Small Changes, Big Impact

One of the most common mistakes executives make is attempting massive AI overhauls without clear, measurable milestones. The reality is that AI transformation does not happen overnight. The smartest approach is to start small, prove AI's value quickly, and then scale up.

Consider how Starbucks implemented AI in its operations. Instead of launching an ambitious, company-wide AI transformation from day one, the company started with small, high-impact AI applications. Starbucks used AI-driven predictive analytics to personalize customer recommendations and improve inventory management, ensuring that stores stocked the right products at the right time. These small but impactful AI implementations led to increased customer engagement, reduced waste, and improved operational efficiency—all within the first few months.

For executives looking to implement AI in the first 90 days, the priority should be to identify business functions where AI can drive immediate value. Some quick wins include:

- Enhancing customer experience through AI-powered chatbots, automated customer support, and personalized recommendations.

- Optimizing operations by implementing AI-driven demand forecasting, supply chain automation, or intelligent scheduling.

- Improving decision-making by deploying AI-powered data analytics to provide real-time insights for leadership teams.

By focusing on high-impact, low-risk AI initiatives, executives can demonstrate value early, securing internal buy-in and setting the stage for broader AI integration.

Building an AI-Ready Team and Culture

No AI initiative can succeed without the right people, processes, and mindset in place. In the first 90 days, executives must assess their organization's AI readiness, identifying skills gaps, internal resistance, and areas that need upskilling. AI is not just about hiring data scientists—it's about ensuring that every department understands how AI can enhance their work.

For instance, Goldman Sachs, a firm deeply entrenched in financial services, faced resistance when AI was first introduced into its trading operations. Many senior traders feared AI would replace their roles. Instead of forcing an AI transition, Goldman Sachs focused on educating employees about AI's role as an enabler, not a disruptor. They provided training programs, AI literacy workshops, and internal AI accelerators, ensuring that employees were part of the AI journey rather than sidelined by it.

Executives must take a similar approach by:

- Identifying internal AI champions — leaders within different departments who can advocate for AI adoption.

- Providing AI education and training — ensuring employees at all levels understand how AI can support their work.

- Addressing resistance with transparency — explaining AI's role clearly and proactively managing concerns.

When employees see AI as a tool for empowerment rather than displacement, AI adoption becomes smoother, and organizational buy-in increases.

Laying the Foundation for AI Scalability

While the first 90 days are about securing quick wins, they should also lay the groundwork for long-term AI success. Many companies make the mistake of implementing AI in silos, leading to fragmented, unscalable solutions. To avoid this, executives should focus on:

- Building AI governance frameworks to ensure ethical, transparent, and responsible AI use.

- Establishing cross-functional AI teams to integrate AI seamlessly across departments.

- Aligning AI with long-term business goals, ensuring that AI investments contribute directly to growth and innovation.

A powerful example of scalable AI adoption is Walmart's use of AI in retail operations. Initially, Walmart used AI for simple inventory tracking and demand forecasting. However, because it had built a scalable AI infrastructure, it was able to expand AI's role into automated checkout, customer service chatbots, and even AI-powered supply chain logistics. Walmart's AI journey started with small, strategic wins—but by ensuring that every AI initiative aligned with its broader business strategy, it scaled AI adoption across the entire enterprise.

The Executive's AI Action Plan for the First 90 Days

In the first three months of AI adoption, the goal is not perfection—it's momentum. AI-driven executives recognize that AI is a continuous journey, not a one-time implementation. By focusing on mindset shifts, quick wins, team readiness, and scalability, they can lay the foundation for a sustainable AI transformation that delivers both immediate impact and long-term success.

AI is no longer a luxury or an experimental technology—it is a business imperative. The executives who act decisively within their first 90 days will position their organizations for long-term leadership in the AI-driven future.

Chapter 12: Amplifying Human Potential – AI's Role in Supercharging Team Performance

For decades, the dominant narrative around AI has centered on automation — machines replacing human jobs, businesses becoming less dependent on human workers, and industries being reshaped by intelligent systems. But in reality, AI's most transformative role is not in replacing humans but in augmenting their capabilities, enhancing decision-making, and unlocking higher levels of performance. AI-driven leaders understand that the real power of AI lies in amplifying human potential, enabling teams to work smarter, faster, and more effectively.

In today's fast-moving business landscape, organizations that successfully integrate AI into their teams will have a significant competitive advantage. AI is not about replacing people — it's about empowering them to do more, create more, and achieve more. This chapter explores how executives can use AI to enhance workforce productivity, optimize collaboration, and enable employees to operate at peak performance.

AI as an Enabler, Not a Replacement

One of the greatest misconceptions about AI is that it will inevitably replace jobs at scale. While it's true that AI automates repetitive tasks, it also creates new opportunities by eliminating inefficiencies, reducing cognitive overload, and allowing people to focus on higher-value work.

Consider the example of AI-powered legal research tools like ROSS Intelligence, an AI-driven system that scans thousands of legal documents in seconds, providing lawyers with relevant case laws, precedents, and arguments. In traditional legal settings, junior associates would spend countless hours sifting through legal texts — a task that AI can now accomplish in minutes. But rather than making these professionals obsolete, AI frees them up to focus on strategy, client interaction, and courtroom performance.

Similarly, AI is transforming the healthcare sector. At Mayo Clinic, AI-driven diagnostic tools assist radiologists by highlighting potential abnormalities in scans. These systems do not replace doctors; instead, they reduce diagnostic errors, speed up decision-making, and allow doctors to focus on treatment rather than time-consuming analysis. This augmentation of human expertise is what makes AI indispensable — not as a replacement for human talent, but as a force multiplier that enhances precision, efficiency, and innovation.

Optimizing Team Collaboration and Productivity

In a world where hybrid and remote work have become the norm, AI has emerged as a key enabler of seamless collaboration, communication, and productivity. Organizations that leverage AI-driven tools can streamline workflows, reduce unnecessary administrative burdens, and improve how teams interact and execute projects.

Take Salesforce's AI-powered assistant, Einstein. This system analyzes customer interactions, predicts sales trends, and even suggests the best course of action for sales teams. Instead of spending hours on manual data entry and analysis, sales professionals can focus on closing deals, building relationships, and driving revenue growth.

In the world of creative collaboration, tools like Grammarly and Jasper AI help writers, marketers, and content creators refine their messaging, improve clarity, and generate ideas at scale. By handling the more repetitive aspects of content creation, these AI tools allow teams to focus on creativity, storytelling, and strategic thinking—tasks that only humans can truly excel at.

Even within internal operations, AI is reshaping project management and team coordination. AI-driven platforms like Trello, Asana, and Monday.com use machine learning to predict project bottlenecks, assign tasks based on workload balance, and automate repetitive follow-ups, ensuring that teams remain productive without getting bogged down by administrative overhead.

Executives who recognize AI as a team accelerator rather than a job eliminator will be best positioned to create high-performing, AI-empowered organizations. The key is to integrate AI tools that complement human skills, not compete with them.

Enhancing Employee Decision-Making with AI Insights

Beyond automation and productivity, AI plays a crucial role in enhancing human decision-making by providing employees with data-driven insights, predictive analytics, and real-time recommendations. Whether it's sales forecasting, risk assessment, or market trend analysis,

AI ensures that decision-making is no longer based on guesswork—it's informed by precise, data-backed intelligence.

For example, Unilever uses AI to analyze recruitment data and identify candidates who are the best fit for its corporate culture. Instead of relying solely on intuition, hiring managers can make smarter, bias-free hiring decisions based on AI-driven assessments, ensuring a more diverse and high-performing workforce.

In finance, JPMorgan Chase's COiN platform leverages AI to review legal documents and contracts, drastically reducing the time spent on manual analysis. This AI-driven system allows analysts and legal teams to make faster, more accurate decisions while focusing on high-level strategy rather than paperwork.

When executives empower their teams with AI-driven insights, employees can make better choices, react to market shifts faster, and operate with greater confidence. AI doesn't just support human judgment—it enhances it, ensuring that leaders and employees make the best decisions with the best available information.

The Future of Work: AI as a Collaborative Partner

As AI adoption accelerates, the most successful organizations will be those that view AI not as a separate entity but as an integrated part of the workforce. AI should be seen as a collaborative partner that works alongside employees, augmenting their abilities, reducing inefficiencies, and allowing them to focus on high-impact tasks.

A perfect example of this is IBM's AI-driven HR assistant, Watson, which helps HR teams manage talent acquisition, employee engagement, and workforce planning. By analyzing employee feedback, predicting turnover risks, and suggesting personalized career development paths, Watson enables HR professionals to focus on building stronger relationships with employees rather than administrative processes.

Companies like Amazon and Tesla are also leveraging AI-powered robotics to enhance human labor rather than replace it. In Amazon's fulfillment centers, AI-driven robots handle repetitive packaging and sorting tasks, while human workers focus on managing logistics, quality control, and problem-solving—areas where human intelligence is irreplaceable.

AI-Powered Leadership: Preparing Teams for an AI-Driven Future

For executives, the challenge is not just integrating AI into existing workflows but preparing their teams for AI-driven collaboration. AI literacy and upskilling will be critical for ensuring that employees feel empowered rather than threatened by AI.

This means investing in:

- AI training programs that educate employees on AI's capabilities and limitations.

- Cross-functional AI teams that encourage collaboration between AI specialists and domain experts.

- Ethical AI frameworks that ensure AI is used responsibly and transparently within the organization.

Executives who actively prepare their teams for AI integration will create workforces that are more innovative, adaptable, and future-ready. AI-driven leadership is not about choosing humans or AI—it's about creating a workplace where humans and AI work together to achieve unprecedented levels of performance.

AI is a Competitive Advantage for Talent

AI is no longer a futuristic concept—it is a present-day necessity. Organizations that successfully integrate AI into their teams will outperform competitors, attract top talent, and redefine what high-performance teams look like.

Executives who embrace AI as a force for human augmentation rather than replacement will lead organizations that are smarter, more agile, and better equipped for the future of work. The real power of AI lies not in eliminating jobs, but in amplifying human creativity, intelligence, and strategic thinking—unlocking the full potential of every employee and every team.

Chapter 13: AI and Organizational Change – Managing Transitions with Confidence

AI adoption is no longer a matter of if—it's a matter of when and how. Yet, despite AI's immense potential to transform industries, executives often struggle with managing the organizational changes required to integrate AI successfully. The challenge isn't just technological; it's deeply human. Resistance to change, fear of job displacement, and uncertainty about AI's role create friction that can stall progress.

The most successful AI-driven organizations are those that approach AI implementation as a cultural shift, not just a technology upgrade. Executives who lead with confidence and clarity can navigate AI transitions more effectively, ensuring that employees embrace AI as an enabler rather than an existential threat.

The Human Side of AI: Overcoming Resistance and Fear

One of the biggest hurdles in AI adoption is the psychological resistance that employees feel when confronted with new technology. This is not a new phenomenon—history is filled with examples of workforce anxiety during technological revolutions. When ATMs were introduced, bank tellers feared job losses, yet their roles evolved into customer-focused advisory positions. When computers replaced typewriters, administrative staff had to upskill, but those who adapted thrived.

Today, AI presents a similar transition. Employees often assume that AI is designed to replace them when, in reality, it is built to augment their capabilities. Leaders must communicate this effectively. When AI-driven automation was introduced at IBM's HR department, employees initially feared job losses. However, executives emphasized that AI would handle repetitive, data-intensive tasks, freeing HR professionals to focus on strategic workforce planning and employee engagement. As a result, job satisfaction increased, and AI was embraced rather than resisted.

Executives must foster AI literacy within their organizations. Employees need to understand how AI works, its limitations, and how it can enhance their roles. Education, transparency, and involvement are key. When Amazon integrated AI-powered robotics into its warehouses, it invested heavily in upskilling workers, ensuring that employees were trained to manage, collaborate with, and oversee AI-driven processes rather than fear them.

Leading AI-Driven Change: A Strategic Framework

Navigating AI-driven change requires more than just rolling out new technology—it requires a structured approach to transformation.

Executives must align AI initiatives with business strategy, create a culture of adaptability, and manage transitions with precision.

A powerful example of AI-driven change management comes from General Electric (GE). When GE implemented AI-driven predictive maintenance across its industrial operations, the transition wasn't just about technology—it was about reshaping workflows, redefining job roles, and ensuring AI was integrated seamlessly into daily operations. To achieve this, GE's leadership adopted a three-phase AI transition framework:

1. Pilot and Prove – Instead of a company-wide AI rollout, GE tested AI in controlled environments, proving its value to employees before expanding adoption.

2. Engage and Educate – Employees were involved in AI implementation decisions, ensuring they understood how AI would support, not replace, their work.

3. Scale and Sustain – Once AI's benefits were clear, the company scaled its use, embedding AI into company culture and long-term strategy.

By following a similar structured approach, executives can ensure that AI adoption is gradual, well-communicated, and aligned with employee needs, reducing resistance and increasing acceptance.

AI as a Catalyst for Organizational Agility

AI adoption is not just about automating processes—it's about making organizations more agile, adaptive, and resilient. Companies that successfully integrate AI gain the ability to respond to market shifts faster, innovate continuously, and future-proof their operations.

A prime example is Netflix, which uses AI-powered recommendation engines to personalize content for users. But beyond that, Netflix's AI-driven approach extends to content production, market analysis, and customer engagement. The company continuously adapts based on AI insights, making it one of the most agile and customer-centric businesses in the world.

Similarly, Tesla's AI-driven approach to vehicle design, manufacturing, and autonomous driving enables it to pivot rapidly, introducing software updates and innovations at an unprecedented pace. Tesla's agility comes from a leadership mindset that embraces AI as a core driver of continuous evolution, rather than a static tool.

Executives must recognize that AI is not a one-time transformation — it's an ongoing process. The ability to adapt, iterate, and evolve with AI is what will set future-ready organizations apart from those stuck in the past.

AI Leadership is Change Leadership

AI-driven leadership is not about deploying technology — it's about guiding people through transformation. Managing AI transitions requires vision, empathy, and adaptability. The best executives approach AI adoption as an organizational evolution, not just a technical implementation.

Companies that embrace AI with confidence, clarity, and a people-first approach will not only enhance operational efficiency but also build organizations that are smarter, more agile, and better positioned for the future. AI is not the enemy of human potential—it is the key to unlocking it.

Chapter 14: Scaling AI – A Practical Guide to Moving from AI Adoption to AI Mastery

The path to AI mastery doesn't end with initial adoption — it only begins there. Most organizations experience an early rush of enthusiasm after launching pilot AI projects, but few manage to sustain the momentum needed to scale AI across functions, markets, and business units. True value lies not in isolated experiments, but in building AI into the core operating system of the enterprise. To achieve this, executives must move beyond viewing AI as a tool or initiative and begin treating it as a strategic competency — one as essential as finance, marketing, or operations.

Scaling AI is fundamentally a leadership challenge. It requires rethinking organizational structures, workflows, and mindsets. It demands patience, resilience, and a deep commitment to transformation. Yet, when done right, scaling AI can unlock exponential growth, market differentiation, and long-term competitive advantage.

From Experiments to Enterprise-Wide Impact

Most AI journeys begin with experimentation — proof-of-concept pilots in limited environments. These early efforts are often led by IT or data science teams, targeting well-scoped problems such as automating invoice processing, predicting customer churn, or enhancing fraud detection. But moving from these early wins to enterprise-wide scale requires deliberate orchestration.

Take the case of Airbus, the European aerospace giant. When Airbus began integrating AI, it didn't stop at individual solutions. After initial successes in using AI for predictive maintenance on aircraft engines, the company established an internal AI Center of Excellence to standardize best practices, share infrastructure, and support business units company-wide. This deliberate scaling process helped Airbus build over 400 AI applications across engineering, procurement, manufacturing, and customer service—each one feeding into a connected digital ecosystem.

Scaling also means democratizing AI beyond technical teams. It's not enough for data scientists to own AI; business leaders, product managers, operations directors, and marketers all need to understand and apply it in their domains. This was the philosophy at McKinsey & Company, where AI is taught not just to technologists but also to client-facing consultants. The firm invested in company-wide AI literacy programs, ensuring that even those without technical backgrounds could speak fluently about machine learning, natural language processing, and AI ethics.

This cross-functional approach transforms AI from a specialized capability into a shared organizational language. It ensures that the business value of AI isn't trapped in technical silos, but is embedded in how decisions are made, how strategies are formed, and how services are delivered.

Infrastructure, Governance, and Trust

For AI to scale, organizations must lay the right foundations — technological, organizational, and ethical. That begins with infrastructure. Scalable AI requires robust data pipelines, cloud platforms, APIs, and MLOps (machine learning operations) frameworks that allow models to be developed, deployed, monitored, and updated at scale. It also demands a flexible architecture that integrates with existing enterprise systems, rather than existing in isolation.

Yet, technical infrastructure is only one part of the equation. Just as critical is the governance framework that guides AI use — who owns AI strategy, how models are validated, what safeguards are in place to protect privacy and prevent bias. Without governance, scaling AI becomes chaotic, risking ethical failures and regulatory backlash.

Consider JP Morgan Chase, which developed a comprehensive AI governance framework covering model development, validation, and explainability. The bank created AI risk management protocols similar to those used in credit or market risk — ensuring AI systems are regularly audited, tested for fairness, and reviewed for unintended consequences. This governance not only builds trust internally, but also reassures regulators and customers.

Trust, in fact, is the bedrock of scalable AI. Employees must trust that AI won't replace them but will empower them. Customers must trust that AI enhances their experience without compromising their privacy. Executives must trust that AI decisions are reliable, explainable, and accountable. Building this trust takes time — and constant reinforcement through communication, transparency, and a commitment to human oversight.

Cultivating AI Maturity Across the Enterprise

AI mastery is not just about using more AI—it's about using it more wisely. Mature organizations don't chase every shiny new algorithm. Instead, they integrate AI into strategic objectives, customer value propositions, and core processes.

Take Procter & Gamble, a global leader in consumer goods. P&G uses AI to optimize everything from supply chain operations to product formulation. In one example, it used machine learning models to reduce packaging waste and improve sustainability outcomes—aligning AI capabilities with larger corporate responsibility goals. What's important here is not just the tech, but the clarity of purpose: AI serves business values, not the other way around.

True AI maturity also shows up in agility. At Alibaba, AI is embedded in decision-making processes from top to bottom. Algorithms are used not just in e-commerce recommendations, but in inventory management, logistics, pricing, and even human resources. What allows this fluidity is Alibaba's platform mindset—AI tools are modular, easy to integrate, and designed to evolve.

Ultimately, scaling AI is a journey of cultural transformation. It requires that organizations adopt a mindset of continuous learning, experimentation, and feedback-driven iteration. Leaders must create safe spaces for innovation while holding teams accountable for measurable results. The move from adoption to mastery is not linear— it's dynamic, requiring recalibration and recommitment at every stage.

The goal is not just to have AI projects. The goal is to become an AI-powered organization—one where data-driven insight fuels every decision, where teams are empowered by intelligent systems, and where innovation is not occasional, but operational.

With the right leadership, infrastructure, trust, and culture, this is not only possible — it is inevitable.

Conclusion

The Future of Leadership: Redefining Executive Excellence in the AI Era

We are standing at a pivotal crossroads in the evolution of leadership. Artificial Intelligence is no longer a futuristic concept relegated to research labs or tech startups—it has become a force shaping every industry, every decision, and every executive's strategic agenda. The emergence of AI is not merely an add-on to existing leadership models; it is redefining what it means to lead in the 21st century.

Executive excellence in this new era will not be defined by how much technology a leader understands, but by how well they translate technological potential into meaningful outcomes—for their people, their organizations, and the world. The AI-driven and AI-savvy executive is not just fluent in emerging technologies; they are visionaries who can sense where the future is heading and marshal resources, talent, and culture toward that horizon.

In many ways, AI is a mirror that reflects the values and priorities of those who wield it. It can either amplify short-term gains or catalyze long-term transformation. It can entrench bias or advance fairness. It can dehumanize processes or elevate human potential. The difference lies in the leadership behind the systems. In how decisions are made. In how risks are weighed. In how people are treated in a world increasingly guided by algorithms.

Take a lesson from the likes of Satya Nadella, whose reinvention of Microsoft wasn't just about cloud and AI—but about building a culture of empathy, learning, and curiosity. Or Arvind Krishna, who led IBM through a pivotal transformation by marrying AI with responsible stewardship and deep industry insight. These leaders show us that the heart of AI leadership isn't just intelligence — it's wisdom.

The AI-savvy executive doesn't fear disruption — they initiate it. They don't rely on playbooks — they write new ones. They are not passive recipients of innovation — they are active architects of the future. And they are defined not by how much they know, but by how they empower others to thrive in an increasingly intelligent world.

The next generation of leadership will belong to those who see AI not as a threat to be managed or a buzzword to be exploited — but as a partner in progress. It will belong to those who lead with clarity, conviction, and courage. Leaders who realize that human intuition and machine intelligence are not rivals, but collaborators in shaping the future of value creation, purpose-driven growth, and inclusive innovation.

As you step forward into this AI-powered future, remember: the most powerful algorithm in any organization is leadership itself. And the most valuable code is the one written not in Python, but in vision, ethics, and empathy.

The era of the AI-driven and AI-savvy executive has arrived. The question is no longer whether you will adapt to it — but how boldly you will lead through it.

Apendix

AI Vocabulary for Executives

To empower your ongoing conversations and decision-making, here's a brief glossary of key AI terms:

- Machine Learning (ML): Algorithms that learn patterns from data to make predictions or decisions.

- Natural Language Processing (NLP): Enables machines to understand and interpret human language.

- Neural Networks: Algorithms modeled after the human brain that are used in deep learning.

- Model Training: The process of feeding data into an algorithm so it learns from it.

- Inference: The process of using a trained model to make predictions on new data.

- Explainability (XAI): Techniques that make AI decisions understandable to humans.

- Bias in AI: Systematic errors in AI output caused by biased data or model design.

- MLOps: Operational practices for deploying, monitoring, and maintaining ML models in production.

- Generative AI: AI systems that create content such as text, images, or code.

AI Governance Checklist for Executives:

1. Do we have an AI ethics framework?

2. Who is responsible for model validation and performance tracking?

3. Are our data sources diverse and representative?

4. Do we offer AI literacy training to business leaders and employees?

5. Are we aligned with local and international AI regulations?

About the Author

Silva Nash is an internationally recognized AI strategist, executive coach, and keynote speaker who helps leaders harness the transformative power of artificial intelligence to drive sustainable growth and future-proof their organizations.

With over 13 years of experience at the intersection of technology, business, and leadership, Silva Nash has worked with Fortune 500 companies, government agencies, and start-ups alike, guiding them through digital transformation and AI integration.

A frequent contributor to major publications and a trusted voice on the ethics and strategy of AI adoption, Silva Nash blends deep technical insight with real-world executive pragmatism. Their approach centers on empowering leaders—not just to understand AI, but to lead with it.

When not advising C-suites or writing about the future of work, Silva Nash is deeply passionate about mentoring the next generation of AI-literate leaders and ensuring that technology serves humanity, not the other way around.

www.ingramcontent.com/pod-product-compliance
Lightning Source LLC
Chambersburg PA
CBHW071006050326
40689CB00014B/3509